Be a Great Thinker

Book Four

Aristotle

The Philosopher's Philosopher

Written By

Adrienne Roth

ISBN: 979-8-9861552-2-7

Contents

An Introduction to the Philosopher Aristotle 1

Who Is Aristotle? 3

Aristotle The Educator 9

Aristotle and The Study of Biology 16

Aristotle Aristotle's Four Causes or the Reasons Why
Things Exist 25

Aristotle and the Study of the Laws of Logic 30

Aristotle and Metaphysics or the First Philosophy 35

Aristotle and the Theory of the Soul................................. 42

Aristotle and Politics... 46

Aristotle – The Greatest Influencer of All Time.............. 54

Some Takeaways about Aristotle 63

Bibliography.. 65

Book Illustrations... 70

About the Author 74

An Introduction to the Philosopher Aristotle

"There is no great genius without some touch of madness."

- Aristotle

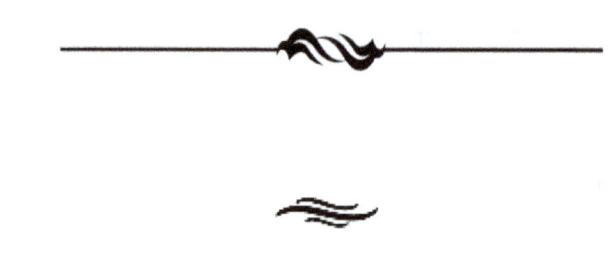

A ristotle is one of the best-known ancient Greek philosophers. The other philosophers of ancient Greece include Socrates, Plato, and Pythagoras. But more than his compatriots, Aristotle is often regarded as Western philosophy's most significant intellectual figure.

Aristotle started his journey into philosophy as a student and a teacher at Plato's Academy in Athens, Greece. Aristotle also taught famous and influential future kings and had a well-known educational institution that he started later in his life. It is through his education institution that Aristotle's brilliance shined.

Throughout his life, Aristotle authored a large number of works. He created a multitude of philosophical concepts and scientific systems. His ideologies and positions touched upon every subject, ranging from biology to logic, metaphysics, mathematics, and politics, as well as studies on life, death, love, and the soul.

Much of what Aristotle wrote and taught became the framework for scholars, philosophers, and scientists throughout the last few centuries. He influenced many great minds from the Medieval era to the Renaissance, the Reformation, and the Enlightenment. His concepts have remained immensely popular with modern philosophers and scientists.

Many people consider Aristotle as their favorite philosopher. Aristotle is so popular because he did not perceive the world in an esoteric manner, as did histeacher Plato. His concepts were always far easier to comprehend. They were written in a no-nonsense fashion, tailored to the average mind, using common-sense methods. For this reason, his ideologies were followed by many people of diverse cultures and backgrounds.

Those who discover Aristotle are amazed by the scope of all he has accomplished and written. You can begin the journey into philosophy and science by examining what he conceived.

We hope you will go further into your discovery of Aristotle, who was indeed the Philosopher's Philosopher. We can only touch upon a small portion of Aristotle's work. What you will get from this book is simply a taste of his concepts and philosophies.

Who Is Aristotle?

"Knowing yourself is the beginning of all wisdom."

- Aristotle

A ristotle was born in 384 BCE in Macedonia, located in Northern Greece.

Aristotle's father, Nicomachus, was very well-connected in ancient Greek society. He was a physician to King Amyntas III of Macedonia. King Amyntas was the grandfather of Alexander the Great.

Aristotle's father died when he was a young boy. Not much is known about Aristotle's mother; she likely died when he was an infant. Aristotle became an orphan at a young age.

Aristotle's brother-in-law, Proxenus of Atarneus (who married Aristotle's older sister, Armineste), became the young boy's guardian. He remained his guardian until Aristotle turned seventeen. At seventeen, Aristotle was sent to Athens for higher education. Athens, at that time, was considered the academic center of the universe. Aristotle enrolled and was accepted into the great philosopher Plato's Academy. He immediately excelled at the Academy. He remained there for 20 years, going from being a prized student to one of its exalted professors.

Aristotle left the Academy shortly after Plato's death. He did not want to stay when Plato's nephew Speusippus took over the Academy. Aristotle and Speusippus butted heads constantly, especially on how the Academy should be run.

Aristotle decided not only to leave the Academy but to leave Athens altogether.

Aristotle moved to Assus, which was located in Anatolia (which is now modern-day Turkey). The ruler of Assus, Hermias, was a friend and colleague of Aristotle from their days at Plato's Academy. Aristotle married Hermias' ward, Pythias. This marriage made Hermias Aristotle's father-in-law. After his marriage to Pythias, Aristotle became a prized advisor to Hermias. At one point, Aristotle helped Hermias negotiate a political alliance with Macedonia. The problem with this alliance was that it made Persia quite angry. Because of that, the King of Persia arrested Hermias and put him to death.

When Aristotle lived in Assus, he spent much of his time on the island of Lesbos. While on that island, Aristotle began doing a great deal of biological and scientific research on the island's animals, insects, and marine life. He documented his extensive research in two works. One was on the physical make-up of these animal species, and the other was on the generations of the animals.

Aristotle's research on animals was groundbreaking. This kind of research on animal biology was never completed before, especially not in such detail and scope. Aristotle classified over 500 species of animals. He documented how they lived, what they ate, how they worked, and how they reproduced. But some of his work was criticized and met with doubt and skepticism from his colleagues. Although they weren't readily praised when he presented them, they have stood up over the centuries. We will dive deeper into his biological discoveries later in this book.

Aristotle knew he needed to learn more about the animals he studied and documented. He fully accepted his ignorance. But he also worked hard to prove his theories by putting together evidence and facts. He may have been controversial in his time, but he used solid methodology to prove his theories.

In 342 BCE, Macedonia's leader Philip II asked Aristotle to return to his hometown. He put Aristotle in charge of educating his thirteen-year-old son Alexander, so Alexander was one of Aristotle's students. Aristotle also taught lessons to two other future kings while tutoring Alexander. One of those students was Ptolemy,  Alexander's companion, who eventually became the king of Egypt. The other student was Cassander, another good friend of Alexander's, who would, for a time, be the King of Macedonia.

Aristotle remained in charge of Alexander's education until Alexander ascended to the throne. He remained in close contact with Alexander throughout his reign as king. As Alexander began conquering the region, he eventually got the moniker "Alexander the Great." For most of Alexander's reign, Aristotle remained very influential in Alexander's life. He went from being his teacher to an essential advisor to the young ruler. Aristotle helped Alexander work through complex diplomatic and political conflicts. Alexander was very bright. He always read books while on his different wartime and diplomatic campaigns. He always remembered Aristotle's teachings. Alexander loved reading, art, and culture, much of which came from Aristotle's influence and lessons.

One of the things Aristotle influenced Alexander to accomplish was to encourage him to conquer Persia. Aristotle was not a fan of the Persians, especially since they killed his friend Hermias. Aristotle also believed in "Greek exceptionalism." This played a significant role in how he counseled Alexander in politics and the world. Aristotle's influence impacted Alexander's vision of a new global society.

But eventually, Alexander began to move away from Aristotle's influence and ideologies. He became crueler and more deliberate in his conquests. How Alexander changed his view of the world and, in turn, began to shift away from Aristotle's influence disturbed Aristotle deeply. Alexander wanted Aristotle to follow him into battle. But Aristotle wanted none of that. Instead, he encouraged his nephew Callisthenes to ride with Alexander. Callisthenes was the first person to chronicle Alexander's military successes.

Alexander went on what he termed a "war of revenge" against the enemies of Greece and Macedonia. At first, Aristotle likely approved of this war, but soon Alexander's personality changed. When Alexander liberated Persia in the Battle of Gaugamela, he chose to stay in the east and never returned to Macedonia.

Alexander became enthralled by eastern culture. Aristotle tried to remain a source of influence on the dynamic ruler, but it was challenging as he was so far away. Aristotle used his nephew, Callisthenes, as a go-between. But eventually, Callisthenes fell out of favor with Alexander and was imprisoned. Callisthenes died in prison, although how he died is not fully understood. Some believe that Alexander tortured him to death. In contrast, others think Callisthenes died of disease.

Eventually, Aristotle became more disconcerted and horrified by Alexander's behavior. Their ideological differences became too great a chasm to overcome. When Alexander was poisoned, several people in Macedonia looked at Aristotle as a possible suspect in Alexander's death. But no one could prove Aristotle had a hand in it. Nonetheless, the rumors harmed his reputation.

Aristotle likely learned secondhand about Alexander's death. He may not have had a hand in it, but he probably breathed a sigh of relief over it. This alone would have garnered suspicion, especially from those who remained supportive of Alexander the Great even after his death.

Because of the persistent rumors and accusations, Aristotle was forced to return to Athens in 335 BCE. He established his school in Athens, which he called The Lyceum. Aristotle ran the school for the next twelve years. During that time, his wife, Pythias, died. He remarried soon after and had another son.

While running The Lyceum, Aristotle was quite prolific. He wrote most of his philosophical and scientific works during those years. These works were not meant for wide distribution but as texts and teaching aids for his students. The results were in treatise form—a discourse on a specific topic, just a little longer than the length of an essay but shorter than a book. A treatise involves investigating a particular subject and coming to a conclusion about it. Some of Aristotle's most influential treatises were on the topics of physics, ethics, metaphysics, politics, and the soul.

Aristotle could not wholly escape the persistent accusations against him regarding Alexander's suspicious death. The rumors surrounding his participation in it remained a problem for him later in life. Though he did not suffer any legal consequences over the accusations, he was denounced by political leaders. Eventually, it got to be just too much for Aristotle, and he ultimately had to leave Athens and his beloved school behind, fleeing to his mother's estate in Chalcis, which was located on the island of Euboea in Greece.

Aristotle felt his banishment was similar to what had occurred to the great philosopher and teacher, Socrates. In Socrates' case, the government accused him of corrupting the youth of Athens. Socrates was sentenced to death. Aristotle felt similarly persecuted. Aristotle thought that those in power wanted to silence him. This brought him extreme grief.

Aristotle died soon after taking solace at his mother's estate. His banishment was indeed a death sentence. He was laid to rest next to his wife, Pythias.

Aristotle, ultimately, would not be silenced. Others throughout the world discovered his works long after his death. His words and his teachings became a powerful resource for so many. He eventually accomplished his goal of becoming one of the world's most influential teachers and philosophers.

Aristotle The Educator

> *"The roots of education are bitter, but the fruit is sweet."*
>
> *- Aristotle*

A ristotle was undoubtedly considered the most famous and apt student of his equally renowned teacher, Plato.

As Aristotle finished his academic term at Plato's Academy, he became one of its acclaimed teachers. He excelled in that role, and as he continued in it, he saw himself as more than just a teacher but a respected school administrator. He remained very steadfast in his position at the Academy, staying there for around 20 years, and he would have remained even longer had there not been a conflict with Plato's nephew. The latter took over the Academy after Plato's death. There was just too much friction between the two men, and Aristotle decided it was time to move on to greener pastures elsewhere.

While at the Academy, Aristotle often disagreed with his teacher Plato's philosophical concepts. He was partially on board with Plato's Theory of Forms. Plato's abstract theory examined what he conceived of as real, or what is a perception of reality. He inferred in his theory that reality might only be an illusion. This theory didn't jive with Aristotle's view of the world. Aristotle viewed the world more concretely. His mind worked scientifically, and he looked at facts and evidence to support those views, while Plato's concept of the world was somewhat untouchable, even, to some degree, inconceivable. Aristotle was a practical man, grounded in reality, so he could not comprehend all that his teacher Plato devised with his abstract philosophies.

Aristotle and Plato also differed in their views on ethics and happiness. Plato believed that being virtuous and righteous would bring justice and happiness to the world. Plato felt that virtuousness put a person's soul into harmony.

Aristotle believed that happiness resulted from the educational process and was not part of the human soul. On the other hand, Aristotle believed that happiness was more of a result of a person's activities. He thought these activities were characteristically human. Aristotle also believed that happiness came through philosophical contemplation by people who cultivated intellectual and moral virtues throughout their lives.

This debate was essential to expanding one's mind and understanding the world and how others thought. Though Aristotle differed from many of the philosophical ideologies of his teacher, Plato, he respected him. Though they may have disagreed, Plato expected this kind of debate and disagreement from his students. It helped them in their growth as thinking men. This was something that Plato learned from his beloved teacher, Socrates.

Aristotle thought that the role of a teacher was vital, as it was the teacher's responsibility to relay knowledge through systematic teaching. It was a teacher's job to instill a sense of right and wrong in their students. He understood that his students might need to be made aware of the concepts he taught them, and as their teacher, Aristotle knew his students would ultimately benefit from his guidance. In this way, they would learn the idea and then make their own choices based on what they took from it, which was part of their philosophical and ethical studies.

Aristotle maintained a potent influence over all of his students throughout his years of teaching. For many, even after they no longer followed the texts he taught, Aristotle remained very influential with his students, often working with them as an advisor and continuing to offer his advice and wisdom as they continued in life. This way of educating students became dominant in how Aristotle taught his pupils, including his most famous student, Alexander the Great.

Aristotle felt that being educated meant elevating one's social standing. He also felt that education was the foundation of a stable society. And thus, ignorance leads to a shaky or unstable community. His feelings on this have been proven over the centuries.

Aristotle was fifty years old when he started his school, The Lyceum. The Lyceum was in a building that had been used, at one time, as a gymnasium. The gymnasium was likely used by athletes training for competitions in the ancient Olympics.

Aristotle added his touches to the building to enhance his school. He put together an extensive library where he kept many writings and texts for his students to peruse freely and use in their studies. He gathered together many brilliant research students that were called "Peripatetics." This name comes from a cloister peripatus. A cloister is an enclosure surrounded by covered walkways or alleys connected to the school. The cloister was where like-minded people congregated and lived together. It was where the students studied, and they and the faculty would exercise and have fun. The cloister was, for the most part, the center of the school. It is like a courtyard you might find at a high school or college today. The cloister was also where many debates and discussions were held at The Lyceum. It was where all the main activities happened outside the classrooms.

Where Plato's Academy was a more private institution, more like a club than a school, Aristotle's Lyceum was open to the general public. Aristotle never charged a student. He believed in giving all students at The Lyceum a free education, which was highly controversial at the time. Everyone in Greek society paid for their education. It was part of the culture. It was completely out of the ordinary for you not to pay for your education. Your status in society was based on the fact that you could pay to be educated. Changing this showed how Aristotle was a man ahead of his time.

Aristotle felt that making education free and accessible was extremely important, and it was one of his core principles. He believed very firmly that education was the way to enhance the welfare of his society. This is why he built his school. Of course, there were exceptions to whom he would accept into his school. Women and enslaved people were not allowed at The Lyceum. In his opinion, Aristotle felt they were second-class citizens, and women, in particular, were inferior to men.

Aristotle wrote most of his philosophical and scientific concepts while running The Lyceum. These were texts meant mainly to teach his students and to be used at his school. They were a constant work in progress. He continuously updated these texts as he discovered new concepts or came up with new ideas.

Aristotle wrote his material in a very academic manner, even a bit dry, as opposed to the writings of Plato, Socrates, and other philosophers and educators of the day. He wrote his works this way to be more straightforward in his educational approach. This was unlike Plato, who used dialogues, prose, and allegories to explain his concepts. It is why Plato's ideas and philosophies are more abstract than Aristotle's concepts. It is also why more people find they can relate easier to Aristotle than to Plato.

Aristotle was never a published writer like his teacher Plato. Aristotle was more practical, systematic, and disciplined in his work. He was easier to understand, which made more people flock to his ideas, even in subsequent centuries. Until Aristotle, there were no boundaries between scientific and philosophical disciplines. Aristotle changed all of that. He created different fields to help his students learn these often-complex ideologies and concepts. The disciplines he created became the norm. This was especially so when studying Aristotle's works throughout the ensuing generations.

Aristotle divided the sciences into three types. The first type was productive, the second was practical, and the third was theoretical. We will delve into these later in this book.

While teaching and running The Lyceum, Aristotle was still dealing with the headaches and troubles surrounding Alexander the Great. Alexander had gone completely mad as a leader and conqueror. His suspicious death by poisoning stained Aristotle's life and teaching career. The rumors about Aristotle's possible involvement in Alexander's death caused him to leave his life as an educator and go into hiding. Not being able to do the thing he loved the most—being an educator—broke Aristotle's heart and is likely what ended up killing him.

What Aristotle left behind was his library, filled with his works and treatises. They were vast. The works that have survived have been studied by scholars and philosophers and may only be one-fifth of what Aristotle wrote throughout his life. It is believed that Aristotle's works amounted to over one million words. Some scholars and historians think that one million words weren't even close to what it was and that what he wrote was a number too large to comprehend fully.

In the end, Aristotle went from teaching a relatively small group of students (though they were most likely several hundred) to teaching the world his philosophies and scientific concepts. He became one of the world's most outstanding, influential, and prolific educators. His passion for education followed him long after he died. Undoubtedly, this accomplishment would have satisfied him immensely. Aristotle achieved what he could only have dreamed of doing by being one of Western society's most outstanding educators and philosophers. He did it all not with flair but with hard work and a sense of purpose. He became an excellent guide to others who discovered new philosophies and concepts, and we will further examine his tremendous influence on those philosophers and scholars later in this book.

———◆———

Aristotle and The Study of Biology

"Nature does nothing in vain."

- Aristotle

Aristotle accomplished much in his lifetime. One of Aristotle's most outstanding achievements was inventing the scientific study of biology. Aristotle is considered the father of zoology.

Before Aristotle, Greek philosophers spent much of their time contemplating the origins of life. They wrote about human anatomy and how they thought it functioned. Yet these perceptions were based solely on hypotheses rather than a scientific conclusion. Because their ideas of what made humans tick were based on something other than science, the concepts of these early Greek philosophers remained only speculation for quite a long time.

Aristotle wanted to delve deeper into the subject of human and animal biology. His investigations into animal anatomy elevated the study of biology to a new and broader level.

While Aristotle was teaching at Plato's Academy in Athens, he established a friendship with a former Plato student named Theophrastus.

Theophrastus

Later, Aristotle and Theophrastus decided to team up and go to the island of Lesbos to study the island's animal and plant life. Aristotle specialized in the animal, marine, and insect species of Lesbos and the surrounding areas, while Theophrastus put his energies into studying the various plant and tree life. They spent many years completing these studies. They continued these complex studies even when Aristotle moved to Macedonia to teach Alexander.

At first, Aristotle began observing the wildlife of Lesbos—how they behaved, what they ate, and how the island's wildlife lived and reproduced.

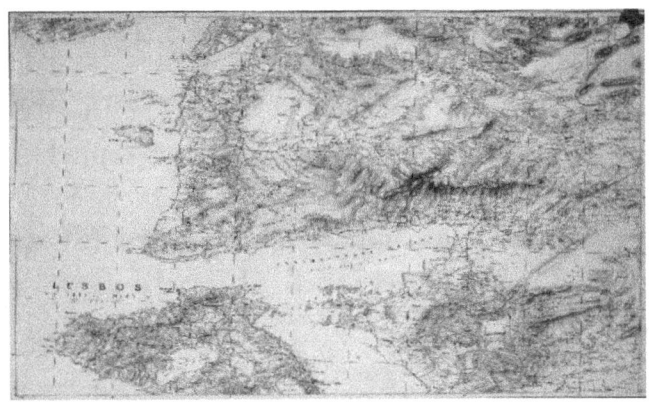

The Island of Lesbos

He would write lengthy notes on his observations as he examined animals in their natural habitat. Later, Aristotle began to dissect these animals, taking note of their biological systems. Aristotle was the first person to observe the inner biology of an animal species.

His discoveries were groundbreaking, and the world of animal biology became a fascinating journey for Aristotle as he went deep into uncharted territory.

During his biological observations, Aristotle named over five hundred species of birds, mammals, fish, insects, and invertebrates like octopuses.

His scientific partner, Theophrastus, conducted similar scientific investigations of the plant and tree life on the island of Lesbos. Both men documented their findings in separate works.

Aristotle used the knowledge he gained from studying under Plato to help construct his biological concepts. He utilized Plato's

Theory of Forms as the base for his scientific ideas. But Plato's Theory of Forms was more of an abstract idea of how the world was formed. It speculated on what was the truth and what was perception. Plato's concept was derived from something other than scientific data. Instead, it explained how different realms of existence could exist on different planes. Aristotle moved the needle with his observations. He went from merely perceiving the truth of existence to proving what and how something existed. Aristotle's observations were based on scientific discoveries. These observations centered on reality rather than the unattainable view of perfection and the perception of what makes a form—Plato's point of view about the world and our existence.

In his scientific observations, Aristotle described five biological processes that pertained to all life on earth. These included metabolism, temperature regulation, information processing, embryogenesis, and inheritance.

The metabolic process describes how an animal breaks down the food it eats and turns it into a source of energy that keeps the cells in its body functioning correctly. Aristotle examined the biological processes that govern how an animal's body functions, from what it eats to how the food it ate generated power in its body and how animals eliminate waste. After observing this, he conceived of the metabolic system, writing about it in his citation, "The Parts of Animals." Aristotle compared the conception of the metabolic system of an animal to the branches of a tree. He perceived each branch as material that moves or is used by the body. These branches include hair, teeth, bones, flesh, lard, fat, and blood.

Aristotle's metabolic system was straightforward. Food is taken into the body. Once inside the body, the food is converted into blood and waste. The waste becomes urine, bile, or feces and is discarded from the body. The food that remains behind is now part of the blood. The blood is turned into what he called "element fire," which is released inside the body as heat. The heat becomes energy. The energy is what creates flesh, bones, and cartilage. Whatever heat is not used as energy is stored as fat.

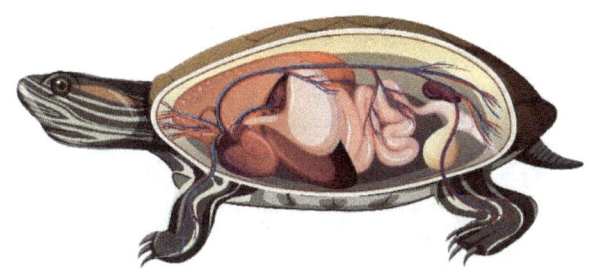

Temperature Regulation was the way Aristotle explained how animals regulate their internal temperature. It also explained how animals breathe.

In the Temperature Regulation system, heat is constantly escaping the body. When food enters the system, it becomes an internal fire that sparks the metabolic process; that inner fire then raises the blood temperature. The inner fire causes the heart's temperature to rise. The rise in the heart's temperature causes the lungs to expand and increase their volume, which makes an animal breathe harder. The breaths the animal takes bring in cool air. The flow of this cool air restores the animal's body temperature to a regular rate. But Aristotle surmised that this only works if the air temperature is cooler than the body temperature. If the air temperature is not cooler, then Aristotle believed that the animal's body temperature would go out of whack. The animal would eventually die from too much heat exposure to its internal organs.

Information Processing is a model that Aristotle created that shows how an animal receives sensory information and uses its limbs, its eyes, its brain, and its body to decoding that information. When Aristotle began this scientific perception, it was only in its beginning stages. At this point in Aristotle's concepts, he wanted to understand how a species might view its world. He later developed a greater understanding of Information Processing as he studied the mind.

Five senses

smell   touch   sight   hearing   taste

Aristotle described embryogenesis as how an animal is formed and how it develops. It starts with the embryo, which develops shortly after fertilization. Aristotle stated that the embryo is the stage that creates the body structures, such as the bones, organs, and connective tissues. It goes from being a one-cell organism, known as the zygote, to a multi-cell organism. The embryo is where the animal develops in the womb. Each species has unique characteristics. The embryo of each species develops at

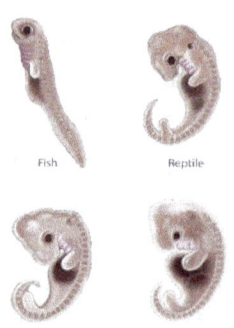

Fish   Reptile

Bird   Human

different lengths of time. Aristotle noted that some embryos form inside the womb, while others develop inside an egg that the mother lays outside her body. He discovered this to be the difference between mammals, who grow embryos in the womb and have live births, and fish, birds, insects, and invertebrates, who give birth to their offspring by laying eggs.

Inheritance was Aristotle's fifth biological process. Inheritance is also known as heredity. The simple definition of inheritance, or heredity, is the passing of specific traits from the parents to their offspring. Inheritance is where the offspring acquires their genetic information from their parents. DNA is part of that genetic information. Though Aristotle did not have a scientific name for DNA, he perceived that the male animal's semen was the primary source of an animal's genetic makeup. According to Aristotle's perception, the mother did not contribute genetic material. The mother's egg was the source of the embryo's nourishment. Her purpose was no more significant than that in Aristotle's summation.

Aristotle's concept of inheritance, or heredity, would eventually spark debate. It would inspire future scholars and scientists to delve further into Aristotle's observations and draw their own scientific conclusions about this biological process. Most of these scientists and scholars went beyond what Aristotle theorized in his early discoveries. The concept of inheritance would develop into the idea of "Nature versus Nurture," which is the debate of whether biology or society is the main factor that determines an animal's fate—or, more aptly, is it one's genetics or is it their environment that makes a difference?

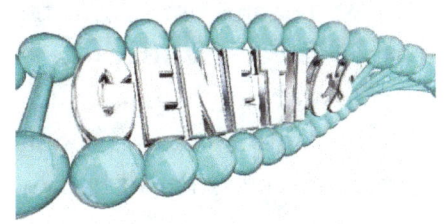

Inheritance also spurred other scientists and scholars, like Darwin, to look at aspects of societal and genetic considerations. "Survival of the fittest" was one of these concepts derived from Aristotle's Inheritance process. Inheritance plays a role in biology and the survival of a species. Those species that can withstand change and can evolve and pass on new and better traits in that evolution will survive. In contrast, other species unable to pass down more vital attributes will eventually die out and go extinct. We know this concept as "natural selection." The concept of "natural selection," or the idea that a weaker bloodline might eventually die out if it cannot evolve, sparked a multitude of controversial ideologies throughout the centuries. It is a concept that still causes arguments to this day.

In his biological studies, Aristotle was incredibly detailed. His style and approach were very new for their time. He organized his data, which enabled him to discover patterns that were never seen before in the natural world, and these patterns helped him better explain what he found. Modern biologists replicated his style, although they went even further with their scientific discoveries. Aristotle documented all of his observations and theories and put these documentations in his works, "The History of Science," and his biological texts, "The History of Animals," "Progression of Animals," "Parts of Animals," and "Movement of Animals." His work "On the Soul" examined the existential view of humans and where that fit into his biological theories.

At the same time, Aristotle's scientific partner, Theophrastus, wrote similar texts on his study of plants, which he called "Enquiry into Plants." Theophrastus was considered the father of botany.

Undoubtedly, Aristotle's study of animal anatomy was the catalyst for future studies of human and animal biology. These works became a base for scholars and scientists in the medieval Islamic world. Aristotle's works were translated into Arabic and Latin and eventually brought into Western Europe, but for a long time, only Aristotle's work, "On the Soul," was taught in universities. Many scientists and scholars who read Aristotle's works on biology concluded that Aristotle had many errors in his theories. They rejected a lot of his work. Scientists and scholars believed his concepts needed to be revised and made more complex. But as the years passed, modern zoologists and marine biologists have concluded that many of Aristotle's observations were right on the money. They utilized his observations as a base for their discoveries. What Aristotle began a couple of millennia ago has remained relevant today. Though some things are outdated and incorrect, when it comes to the study of biology, Aristotle paved the way for biologists, zoologists, and psychologists to develop their conclusions and reach different discoveries through their more introspective observations.

Aristotle Aristotle's Four Causes or the Reasons Why Things Exist

"We think we have knowledge of a thing when we have grasped its cause."

- Aristotle

From as early as he could remember, Aristotle desired to know why certain things occurred in the natural world. It was a fascination for him that he put to practical use in his scientific discoveries.

Aristotle believed that everything had a purpose and followed a specific path. He worked out a way to figure out the cause of each thing. By doing this, he could figure out why a thing existed, how that existence happened, and why it ceased to exist, and this was the circle of life as Aristotle saw it.

Trying to understand why things exist and how they affect the world was quite a daunting task. To help Aristotle answer what seemed difficult to understand, he conceived four causes, which became part of his causal investigations of the natural world.

He wrote about these causes in his treatises, Physics II and Metaphysics V2.

The four causes were:

1. The Material Cause

2. The Formal Cause

3. The Efficient Cause

4. The Final Cause

These four causes were Aristotle's way of applying an explanation to those "why" questions in the physical world, such as "Why does a bird fly?" or "Why can't fish live outside of water?" He used causal investigations the same way another scholar might use the Socratic Method, breaking down the arguments or the theories by asking pertinent questions. Where the Socratic Method pinpoints the view to its most essential element of fact and truth, Aristotle's four causes break down the "why" question by examining it through the four causes to come to a scientific conclusion.

Aristotle conceived that the four causes explain why a thing exists. You can arrive at a plausible scientific explanation when you examine that thing using the four causes.

In the Material Cause, you can examine what that specific thing is made of. Your question may be, "Why does a bird fly?" To answer that question, you must first examine the bird. You will see that the bird has a hollow bone structure. It also has wings that can spread out and catch the air currents, and the bird has feathers. All of these are indicators of why the bird can fly.

In the Formal Cause, you will examine that object or thing (in this case, the bird) and try to understand why it is one type of thing and not something else. In this particular case, when you view the bird, it has feathers. Because of this, the bird adapts to the air better. A bird is not like a fish. A fish, unlike a bird, has gills, so it adapts to the water better. In contemplating these facts, you will see why the bird works in one way while a fish has a separate form of existence in the world. They both work well for their needs, but they cannot exist in each other's worlds because they are not adaptive to those worlds. A fish can't fly, and a bird cannot live in the water; though many birds can swim above water, some fish jump high enough that they seem to be flying. But they are different.

The Efficient Cause shows what led to the creation of the things in question, like what created the bird. In Aristotle's time, scholars and philosophers often questioned how something came into existence. At that point, there was no concrete evidence of evolution, so these philosophers and scholars based their conclusions on existence through their religious beliefs. Aristotle had to deal with this conundrum. He contemplated how a species was created by examining that species. He did this by observing them. His astute conclusions held up for a long time and were later used in scientific research by other scholars.

The Final Cause looks at the usefulness of the thing in question (the bird). What purpose does that thing serve for the world? And what is its end goal? The goal is meant to be objective; it can be translated in these respects. Birds are an essential part of the natural world and vital to its existence. There are several species of birds. Some birds of prey, like falcons, hawks, and eagles, serve their purpose by keeping other species, like rodents, in check. Then there are birds, such as chickens and turkeys. These birds do not necessarily fly, but they serve their purpose by being food for other animals, such as wolves, large cats, and humans. Pigeons also have a purpose. Some pigeons are used for sending notes and messages, which help their human handlers with essential tasks.

Aristotle also felt there were primary and secondary causes. According to Aristotle, the primary reason for our existence is our bodies, organs, tissues, and cells. The secondary cause is made up of the things that make up our bodies. This includes atoms and molecules. Each is important and has its place.

Chance and coincidence can also have a cause. According to Aristotle, coincidence alone does not have a cause.

To make this clearer, here is an example. If you drive down the highway and five cars on that highway all get flat tires at the same highway exit, that could be a coincidence.

Now, if you discover each of those cars got a flat tire by having driven over a sharp object at that exit, this is no longer a coincidence; it is chance. Coincidence does not necessarily have a reason behind it; it just happens. Chance has a reason behind it and will almost always have a cause. Case in point: the cause, in this case, is the sharp object all the cars happened to come in contact with at the highway exit.

The Ancient Greeks felt that cause was pertinent to the law. They could put cause into a legal context to determine who or what was responsible for an incident and, thus, who should be given credit or blame for that cause.

Later, philosopher Francis Bacon used Aristotle's more formal term "law" instead of "cause" when writing his works on the natural sciences. Instead of using the four causes to answer questions about nature, Bacon termed his findings "the laws of nature." By doing this, Bacon advanced Aristotle's four causes into a more reflective scientific method.

Aristotle's Final Cause was also instrumental in the study of evolutionary biology. Another famous scientist, Charles Darwin, used Aristotle's Final Cause in his works on biology and evolution.

Understanding the four causes is a good starting point for understanding Aristotle's grasp of the world and how he conducted his scientific methods. It is also an excellent way to begin questioning the natural world when making discoveries. The four causes are the best way to seek answers to complex scientific questions. It is the way many scientists conduct their research even today.

Here are a few questions to contemplate using Aristotle's Four Causes.

- *Why can some people sing while others cannot?*

- *Do we continually evolve, even in our own lives?*

- *Has science shown ways animals evolved to adapt to a new way of living in the world?*

Aristotle and the Study of the Laws of Logic

"Logic will get you from A to B. Imagination will take you everywhere."

- Albert Einstein

O ne of Aristotle's most significant accomplishments was that he was the first western philosopher to develop a formal reasoning and logic system. He invented deductive Logic, putting the study of Logic into a system where it had never been before his concept. Aristotle was quite proud of this particular accomplishment, and the world considered him the Father of Western Logic.

Aristotle presented his works on Logic in "The Organon." For a very long time, over 2000 years, Aristotle's work on Logic was what all scientists and philosophers followed. It was considered the be-all and end-all of the subject. And not until the 20th century was any significant changes made to Aristotle's study of Logic.

Aristotle considered Logic not as a theoretical science that includes physics, mathematics, and metaphysics but more in line with being a tool that all scientists and science would use to draw their scientific conclusions. Logic has become a discipline.

Aristotle created three laws of Logic.

The first law is the Law of Contradiction.

The Law of Contradiction states that something cannot be both a thing and not a thing simultaneously. For example, a chair cannot be both a chair and not a chair simultaneously, or it cannot be both the color blue and not the color blue simultaneously. Aristotle called this concept a "specified kind" or "specified matter." This concept may be complex to consider. In other words, something cannot be accurate and false at the same time. You can't say, "I love lasagna, but I also hate lasagna." The statement doesn't make sense. It doesn't quite fit logically. Once you do this, it becomes a contradiction and is considered an explicit contradiction.

Another explicit contradiction is "I love my brother and I hate my brother." Logically, you can't feel both feelings at the same time. Now, you can have a love-hate relationship with your brother. And this is not a contradiction because there are things you love about your brother and things you might hate about him. These feelings are positive and negative, but they do not contradict each other.

The second law is the Law of Excluded Middle.

This law states that its opposite must be false for something to be accurate. If you say you are human, you cannot, in turn, say that you are not human. Aristotle conceived that, in this law, you could be only one or the other, not both. Aristotle observed that it was not possible to be and not be something at the same time. This law of Logic prevailed during Aristotle's lifetime and for many years. But this law had flaws. In later and more modern Logic systems, the concept of "Negative as Failure" replaced the Law of Excluded Middle. "Negative as Failure" became the updated version of this law. The current idea is that instead of something being false if it isn't true, as Aristotle conceived of this law, a thing will be considered valid until it is no longer proven to be true. It gives the law more wiggle room. Or, in other words, everything isn't so black or white, right or wrong, this or that. There are gray areas in the modern, updated version of this law.

The Law of Excluded Middle has also been used in arguments related to self-contradiction. In the case of self-contradiction, a person will make an argument that is neither true nor false. When this occurs, it is called a Liar's Paradox.

An example of a Liar's Paradox is when a person says, "Right now, I am telling you a lie." But because that person is known to be a prolific liar, whenever they speak, they lie. When they make this statement that they are telling you a lie, their statement about the lie becomes the truth. Herein lies the paradox. If you think long and hard about it, the Liar's Paradox is mind-blowing.

The third law is the Law of Identity.

Aristotle theorized that accuracy is valid for all purposes if we make a statement that is determined to be accurate. In terms of Logic, this means that everything is itself, not something else. For instance, ice cream is ice cream and cannot be steak. Or rain is rain, and rain cannot be sand. The ice cream and the rain each have a specific identity; they cannot be something else.

You identify yourself as a human. It would be challenging to prove that you are something else. So, you are rightly considered a human. Now, your identity, or how you feel about it, might change, but in this Law of Logic, you will still argue that you are a human and identify as such, so it is what it is.

Logic is complex at its core, with many variables. It is not cut and dry and needs much reflection to contemplate how it manifests in our thinking. Aristotle approached it in a studied and scientific manner by organizing it so it could be understood more concisely.

But that being said, it takes much effort to delve into the various concepts of Logic. Practice the theories. See if you can observe the variables of the Laws of Logic in your world.

Do people contradict themselves when they try to present an argument? You can call them out using the Laws of Logic. Remember, nothing is quite as it seems; nothing is black or white. The world is full of gray areas. Studying Aristotle's Law of Logic will open up the world more for you and help you better understand contradictions and scientific concepts by examining the variables.

———✦———

Aristotle and Metaphysics or the First Philosophy

"The World Is, of course, nothing but our conception of it."

- Anton Chekov

A ristotle's preliminary work in his storied career was on Metaphysics. His work on Metaphysics is considered the first significant discipline in Western Philosophy, and Aristotle's work on this subject is highly regarded in all philosophy.

Aristotle referred to Metaphysics as "wisdom."

Aristotle's work on Metaphysics was highly influential among Greek and Muslim philosophers, scholars of all nations, and philosophers and writers like Dante. Aristotle himself called it "the first philosophy" and a discipline that studies "being as being."

Aristotle wrote his philosophy of Metaphysics in several texts throughout his life. His first works on Metaphysics began with his criticism of his teacher Plato's Theory of Forms. The Theory of Forms is Plato's concept that the physical world, or physical realm, as Plato conceived it, is not the realm we believe it to be but is something we cannot see. These unseen objects are called "forms" and are part of the non-physical essence of all things and, in Plato's conception, are part of actual reality. Plato introduced this concept in his Allegory of the Caves, which tells of prisoners chained up in a cave that is presented with shadows of objects.

The prisoners understand these shadows as authentic or part of their known reality. But the shadows are just illusions. The shadows are part of a different realm, not actual reality, but simply a concept of reality as the prisoners understand it.

Aristotle found an issue with Plato's Theory, as it did not consider the matter of objects or how they might change and evolve. Also, during Aristotle's time, atomists were becoming more prevalent. Atomists are natural philosophers who conceived that everything in the universe comprises atoms. This theory is still considered the predominant ideology in the makeup of all things.

Though during Aristotle's time, atomists did not have a word to describe the chemical compound that made up all things in the universe (i.e., the atom). In the early 1800s, an English chemist named John Dalton coined the term "atom" for the chemical compound that comprised all things.

Aristotle was searching for a way to combine the concepts of Plato and the concepts of the early atomists. Aristotle's Metaphysics adapted Plato's idealism, which was primarily based on mathematics, and put it together with the atomists' materialistic view of the world. That view was based on physics and was a combination of natural sciences and epistemology or the difference between actual knowledge and a straightforward opinion.

Aristotle broke his Philosophy of Metaphysics into three distinct and essential questions. We still use these questions in our study of Metaphysics to this day.

- *What is existence, and what is the substance of things?*

- *How does something exist and yet can change—and why does this happen in the natural world?*

- *What is the way we need to understand the natural world?*

Aristotle sought a deeper understanding of the basis of our existence. He wanted to know what made us tick, why we change and evolve, and what the best and most reliable method was to document and understand this.

When Aristotle was creating his Philosophy on Metaphysics, Greek philosophy was still relatively young. Philosophers like Heraclitus and Parmenides started forming theories based on properly observing the natural world. Though raw and incomplete, their views gave both Plato and Aristotle the basis for their ideologies.

Heraclitus thought the world was constantly changing. It always remained active. Parmenides felt just the opposite of his compatriot. He felt the world never changes and there is just one truth or reality. This is the concept upon which Plato based his idea in the Theory of Forms. Aristotle found fault with this. Instead, he wanted to see the truth between the two competing theories.

After studying Plato's Theory of Forms at Plato's Academy, Aristotle did not find Plato's concept viable. Aristotle speculated that there is a thing, such as a person, possibly a young student, that is born and comes into existence. Now, before the student was born, he did not exist. He was not there as part of the world. But after birth and throughout his young life, the student is here and exists in the world. The student then comes to school, grows up, and becomes an adult. Then one day, the adult student learns to swim. While learning to swim, he can hold his breath underwater for a short time. This feat of controlling one's breath underwater was thought to be something only fish or sea mammals could achieve. Because the student can now hold his breath underwater without harm, he has evolved.

In taking this example of the student who grew up and could swim and hold his breath underwater, Aristotle had to take apart much of the facts surrounding it. First, Aristotle needed to understand how the student came into existence in the first place, how he was created, and how he was born. The second fact was how the student evolved, which could be how he grew up from a child to an adult and a student, and then, as a student, how he managed to train himself to hold his breath underwater for a reasonable time. In reviewing this, Aristotle determined that all things in the universe were made up of two things: form and matter.

In Aristotle's concept, matter is also known as hylomorphism. Aristotle concluded that matter is an object relative to something else, like milk or cream being compared to ice cream or sand being equivalent to glass. Therefore, glass is relative in matter to something akin to a window. Matter can change and evolve. It starts as one thing and then transforms into something else, such as sand becoming glass, and then the glass is turned into a window. Aristotle also stated that we perceive objects based on how we view their matter and how we understand and take it in. We know matter by how they look, feel, taste, and smell. In this way, we begin to understand the matter or the object. As we get to know these objects better through these tactile methods, we can accept them as they change and evolve.

Forms are different from matter. Some might say Forms are existential or beyond our complete comprehension. A form can both exist and not exist at the same time. It is the essence of a thing but not the thing itself. Or, in other words, it is the perception of an item rather than the actual item. So, to some degree, the form is an illusion.

As concerning as the concept of a form may seem, the idea that a form is a "known unknown" means that it can be just about anything you think or want it to be. In this regard, a form can be anything you need help understanding, but it only allows a partial explanation of the form itself.

Medieval philosophers were the most enthusiastic about the concept of form. They applied this concept to their theology or religious doctrine. An example is when the Catholic Theologians used the eucharist's bread and wine as the form of the body and the blood of Jesus. It described an unseeable form or concept of an object that one could taste, touch, and experience. And by doing this, they could bring a deeper spiritual understanding to those who needed to experience something physical to comprehend something more in line with an unseeable form belonging to another realm.

Aristotle also conceived the passive and active intellect in his Philosophy of Metaphysics.

A passive intellect understands things it can see, such as a tree, a house, a dog, or the sky. It understands it because it can perceive it almost without question.

An active intellect takes the objects it perceives and turns that perception into knowledge. The active mind then asks questions like how tall is the tree? Why does the dog bark? Why is the sky blue? In his Philosophy of Metaphysics, Aristotle discusses the human mind and how it works by turning the passive intellect into an active intelligence.

For a time after the fall of the Roman Empire in the 5th century, Aristotle's Philosophy of Metaphysics was lost to the non-Greek-speaking world. It was rediscovered in the 9th century in the Arab-speaking world. Here is where Aristotle's teachings took hold. Many Arabic philosophers and scholars completely embraced Aristotle's ideas on Metaphysics. Then the crusades brought Aristotle's works to the attention of medieval scholars, philosophers, and theologians. From that point on, Aristotle's Philosophy of Metaphysics remained a well-known work. It is still reviewed and studied by modern-day philosophers and scholars.

Here are some very weighty questions that you can consider when contemplating the subject of metaphysics.

- *What is the meaning of life?*

- *What is our place in the universe?*

- *Does the world actually exist?*

- *Why is there something rather than nothing?*

- *Do we have free will?*

- *Does God exist?*

- *Does anything I do matter in the scheme of things?*

By tackling these age-old questions, you enter the true realm of philosophy, as Aristotle and his compatriots have done throughout the centuries. By practicing this type of deep thought, these questions will take you into the essence of philosophy and help form your critical mind.

Aristotle and the Theory of the Soul

"The soul is just the form of a living thing."

- Aristotle

A ristotle's view on the soul is more practical than other philosophers' points of view concerning the soul.

Aristotle wrote about the soul when he wrote about animal biology. Other philosophers, including his teacher Plato, believed the soul was part of our consciousness and the essence of our being, separated from our physical body. Aristotle saw the soul as an integral part of every living being, not a separate form.

Aristotle did not see the soul as something that only humans possessed. He believed that every creature on the planet had a soul. He did not conceive the soul as part of an entity belonging to something such as heaven or hell. Aristotle did not believe in an afterlife. Because of this, he never put the soul in the context of being part of that other kind of existence; this concept was never a consideration for him.

Aristotle considered the soul to be the body's primary, or first, part. For Aristotle, the soul "is not separate from the body," or maybe a more straightforward explanation is that the soul must have a body to exist. It cannot exist separately from the body. The body and the soul must work in tandem, as the soul is vital to the existence of the body.

Aristotle created three different functions for the soul.

The first function is the nutritive soul. Aristotle felt that all living beings needed to be nourished to stay alive. They must take in nutrients to feed their bodies, which will then provide nutrients to the soul. For Aristotle, this was a standard function of all living beings.

The second function of the soul is to be wise. With this function, Aristotle observed that all animals could perceive the environment in which they lived. Some animals can take in their environment through heightened senses, such as the sense of smell or sound. In contrast, other creatures that live entirely in the darkness can use touch or vibrations to function successfully in their environment. Perception also leads to desire, as Aristotle conceived it as part of this function.

The third function of the soul is the rational soul. The rational soul is the part that affects our thinking and our intellect. It touches upon a higher stream of consciousness. Though Aristotle felt all living beings had a soul, not all living beings had this function in their soul. He believed that only higher forms of animal species, such as humans, possessed a rational soul.

Aristotle established a hierarchy in which species on the planet can reign based on how their soul functions. He put humans at the top of this hierarchy, as they possessed all three functions of the soul. Other animals and species were placed lower in order, as their souls functioned at a lower level of intuition and perception of their perspective environments. Plants were on the lowest rung, as they only possessed a nutritive soul.

Aristotle felt that movement, action, thoughts, and desire were all related to the function of the soul and not to other inherent causes. He believed that, in some manner, the soul was the spark or the mechanism that enabled the body to function as perfectly as it did.

Aristotle also felt that the soul helped humans find truth and understanding and was part of how humans found purpose in life.

Aristotle delved deeply into the soul's role throughout his works on the soul. His concept of how the soul works were mainly due to how it relates to the body's essential functions. Modern science has discovered more plausible factors for the various bodily functions that Aristotle wrote about. Over the centuries, there has been pushback on Aristotle's perceptions of the soul. Not all philosophers agreed with Aristotle's perceptions of the body and soul. Yet, in Aristotle's work on this subject, he makes some fascinating and deeply reflective arguments about the soul and its place in our existence.

The concept of the soul has been the subject of intense contemplation by many philosophers and scholars throughout the last several centuries. This particular subject was tackled in many different ways by many great minds. Aristotle's theories on the soul are no more or less valid than those of other philosophers. Aristotle's view of the soul is more grounded in its concept. It is based on what he believed were scientific findings and less on the existential perception of the soul.

- *What is your perception of the soul?*

- *Do you agree with Aristotle that our soul is part of our physical being, or is it separated from our body and an entity in itself?*

- *Do you think other animals, including plants, have a soul? Or do you only believe that human beings have a soul?*

- *Do you think that the soul lives on even after death?*

By grasping what many other philosophers, such as Aristotle, tried to capture in their works, you will understand what makes a living being alive and functioning. *Is the soul a part of that, or is it something beyond that?*

This takes much reflection, but it is a good start to discovering the philosopher inside of you.

———◆———

Aristotle and Politics

"*NOW IT IS EVIDENT THAT THE FORM OF GOVERNMENT IS BEST IN WHICH EVERY MAN, WHOEVER HE IS, CAN ACT BEST AND LIVE HAPPILY.*"

- ARISTOTLE

Another significant achievement attributed to Aristotle is that he created political science. Because of this, many scholars and philosophers have considered Aristotle the father of politics or political science.

Politics played a prominent role in Greek society, but the Greeks of Aristotle's time never considered it a science of any sort. Aristotle changed all of that. He established politics as a compelling branch of science and shifted the thinking around it.

Political science contains various subjects, from international politics to political methodology, economic politics, and comparative politics. Each topic within political science touches upon each type of role a person can take when involved in politics.

Political science measures how prosperous nations and individuals are at governing and creating policies and maintaining economic growth, justice and equality in their society, and overall stability in their country.

Aristotle believed that all societies should have a middle class. He felt that people were happiest under a stable political government where they were free to voice their opinions and share in the common good brought about by their government. Aristotle did not like governments that were materialistic or ruled by fanatic points of view. He believed this type of rule would ultimately lead to the destruction of governments. When Alexander the Great ruled Macedonia, Aristotle saw how his student shifted from being an influential leader to someone more interested in materialistic and selfish ideas. This disturbed Aristotle tremendously, and he shunned Alexander for that disastrous shift in his political leadership.

In early American history, leaders like Adams, Hamilton, and Madison, America's founding fathers, greatly appreciated Aristotle's work. They used his concepts to help craft their new American society. Aristotle's work was a blueprint for a free society of free-thinking men, which unfortunately did not include women or enslaved people in this new ideology. The truth was that including women and enslaved people was never a concept in either Aristotle's or the founding fathers' view of a great society.

Aristotle also believed that ethics and politics went hand in hand. He even went so far as to infer that only people involved in politics were, in the same measure, ethical. He believed that politics aimed to bring out the best in the citizens of a community or nation. These citizens would thereby "be disposed to perform noble action" for their community. It was a very high-minded idea.

Most people today would disagree with Aristotle that politicians are very ethical. Politicians do not enjoy the same high opinion that Aristotle and others in his society bestowed upon them. People of our time regard politicians as corruptible, selfish, and serving their own needs and agendas. Politicians of today appear to not view their constituents with anything but contempt and as a vice to further their political careers. It is a much more cynical viewpoint than the one Aristotle had created in his concepts of politics.

Aristotle felt that studying politics and political science was the best way to understand what makes a good government. He believed the city-state (like Athens) was the highest form of community. Families are the next lowest state. Families form villages, and villages include states. The most basic form of the community is individuals. Individuals form families.

Aristotle believed that a government could be ruled by either one person, a small group of people, or many people at once. Government can work for the good of just one person or the general public's welfare.

If one individual rules a government, it is called a monarchy.

When governments rule for the benefit of one person or a small group of individuals, this type of government is considered tyranny.

If a majority of wealthy landowners rule a government, that type of government is called an aristocracy.

If a government is ruled for the state's best interest and for no one else (which entails minority rule), this type of government is an oligarchy.

Polity is now what we would consider part of a democracy. If a populist government rules, Aristotle called that type of government a polity. Aristotle was not necessarily a fan of polity, as this type of leadership was considered mob rule. In his time, a government run by polity was a less-than-ideal way to rule.

Aristotle viewed leadership by the monarchy as a good option. That is, as long as the leaders or rulers of this type of government were fair. If they were not honest or good rulers, then the outcome of this kind of rule would lead to tyranny. This type of tyranny has occurred far too often in history, where one person will start their authority positively, but after a time, their leadership devolves into something more sinister. The once-beloved ruler becomes too powerful, and that power gets to their heads, and they go crazy. This kind of leadership, again, was how Aristotle saw Alexander's rule and why he ultimately opposed him.

Aristotle had no issue with aristocracies. He honestly felt that when a monarch ruled, if he were a reasonable and fair man, he would do well with his subjects.

But Aristotle's preferred type of government was a constitutional democracy. He liked this type of government because it respected the rights of all people equally, rich or poor, educated or not. He felt that the best-qualified community citizens would maintain the country's leadership in this type of government. And this was what the American founding fathers like Washington, Jefferson, Hamilton, Adams, Franklin, and Madison chose for their new government.

Though it was not the perfect type of government, it was the best option for the American founding fathers. These new political leaders in the United States government did toy with the idea of installing a monarchy, as this was the type of leadership they understood best. Having a constitutional democracy was indeed an experiment that, until that point, had not been tried or succeeded. America had just concluded its war to separate from the very restrictive rule of King George. Of all the founding fathers, Washington was the most opposed to a monarchy. His fellow founding fathers would have been okay if he had ruled as a monarch in his role as president, but Washington had a different notion. He purposely served only two terms as president. This was to keep the leaders fresh and the idea of a constitutional democracy strong, as they had initially planned in their experimental government.

Unfortunately, one of the significant flaws in Aristotle's works on political science is that he justified slavery. Athenian society had many enslaved persons, which was part of the world that Aristotle understood. It was simply part of their culture. Aristotle did not think that slavery was unjust or unfair. He considered enslaved people to be property. He speculated that enslaved people would not be necessary if machines could do menial tasks. But they were merely working machines to him, not flesh and blood. His opinion of enslaved people was harsh. Aristotle felt they were inferior humans with little or no value in society. He believed enslaved people needed to be controlled by a master. Aristotle felt they should not be unchained and were incapable of thinking for themselves. Aristotle believed enslaved people should not be allowed to do what others in his society were allowed to do.

Some American founding fathers also had this same sentiment regarding slavery and enslaved people. In this regard, they also found Aristotle to be a kindred spirit and felt even more encouraged by Aristotle's political ideologies.

Aristotle taught his students political science. Part of what he taught was how to use their words when making speeches, move people into action, and manipulate their feelings on a subject or idea. This type of speech-making is a craft that politicians regularly use to help move people to their way of thinking and win them over with their ideologies by inspiring them to follow them into taking action or encouraging their support by voting for them.

Aristotle called this type of speech rhetoric. He very much thought that, if done well, rhetoric was quite valuable.

Politics has evolved to some degree since Aristotle conceived of political science. Not all political ideologies existed in Aristotle's time, but many of his concepts touch on all sorts of political ideologies and how governments rule today. He brought politics to its core, as he had done with many other subjects.

Here are some questions on politics to ponder.

- *Which political party are your parents or other family members affiliated with?*

- *Which type of political ideology do you think suits your view of the world the best?*

- *Do you like the kind of government that your country has?*

- *If you do not like the kind of government your country has, how would you change it?*

- *Do you follow politics, or does this not interest you?*

- *What type of leader would you be if you had the power to lead a nation? Would you want to hoard all of the power for yourself, or would you want everyone in the country to have a say in how the country is run?*

- *Do you think monarchies should still have a role in governments, or should they be abolished?*

Politics and political viewpoints are very diverse, and how you approach them will help you understand how the world works. Aristotle began understanding this discipline, which is more relevant now in our society than ever, even in Aristotle's day. Understanding politics better and delving into the discipline of political science in the manner in which Aristotle developed it in his works will help you become a better citizen and leader.

———◆———

Aristotle – The Greatest Influencer of All Time

"Linnaeus and Cuvier have been my two gods, though in very different ways; they were mere schoolboys to old Aristotle."

- Charles Darwin

Aristotle had a significant impact on the world. His philosophies, scientific methods, teachings, and concepts influenced many philosophers, scholars, scientists, and others throughout the centuries.

For Aristotle, it all began while he was still alive, with his scientific collaboration with the botanist Theophrastus. Theophrastus' work on plant life pairs well with Aristotle's work on animals. Their scientific studies complimented one another, and they were a good team.

The influence of Aristotle spread to his students:

1. When he taught at Plato's Academy.

2. When he was the teacher to Alexander the Great and his young compatriots.

3. When he opened his university, The Lyceum.

After Aristotle's death, his vast body of work continued. Those who studied what he wrote did not question or challenge his observations. His words were gospel. And this remained until Herophilos of Chalcedon, the first teacher of medicine in Alexandria (a city that Alexander the Great founded and became the capital of Egypt), started to take apart Aristotle's theories.

Herophilos

Herophilos was the first person to study and analyze the brain. He differed from Aristotle's view of the brain. Aristotle felt the brain was a secondary organ used as a cooling agent for the heart. Aristotle also believed that a person's spirit was housed in the brain. He also believed that our intellect derives from our senses, which is where the term "common sense" comes from. But Herophilos discovered that the veins in the brain carried blood, and he deduced that this blood was then moved from the brain to the veins and arteries within the body. Of course, later, we would learn that the heart controlled blood flow, but even so, Herophilos knew the brain was a vital organ. Herophilos also differed from Aristotle in that Aristotle believed that a person's intellect came from their heart. In contrast, Herophilos speculated that it came from the brain. He was the first to differentiate the cerebrum (the most significant part of the brain) from the cerebellum (the smaller, lower section of the brain), which controls our motor and cognitive functions, like speech, and our emotions, like fear, happiness, sadness, and pleasure.

The early Greek Christians played an essential role in preserving Aristotle's work. They took great pains to copy his manuscripts and share them with scholars and theologians. One of the more prominent early followers of Aristotle's works was John of Alexandria, a Christian theologian. He critiqued Aristotle's works on physics, meteorology, the soul, and corruption. His critiques of Aristotle brought him much criticism from the church, though he never experienced that criticism directly, as most of it came after John's death. Like Herophilos, John also differed from many of Aristotle's teachings, especially those on physics. Part of the reason John was criticized was that he pointed out flaws in Aristotle's works on physics. He was alone in doing this, as most of the church revered Aristotle and would never dare review his works with critical eyes. Any criticism of Aristotle was not heard, accepted, or welcomed. At that time, Aristotle was considered the most extraordinary mind in the church.

Not only did the Byzantine and the Greek churches completely revere Aristotle, but he also influenced the early Islamic theologians. A great majority of Aristotle's work was translated into Arabic and studied by Muslim scholars, scientists, and philosophers.

Thomas Aquinas
1225 – 1274

In early medieval times, Thomas Aquinas, who was among the first medieval philosophers and was also widely considered one of the greatest theologians of the Catholic Church, often combined ideas put forth by Aristotle. He added them to the many principles of Christian fundamentalism. Aristotle heavily influenced Aquinas's work. Thomas Aquinas's works are still taught in today's Catholic church, especially by those studying to become priests. Aquinas was made a saint after his death.

By the later medieval era, studying ancient Greek philosophers such as Aristotle was no longer the thing to do. In fact, for several hundred years, the vast majority of the medieval world just stopped even reading, disseminating, or teaching the Greek philosophers. By this point, most of these philosophers' works were written in the ancient Greek language, which most people did not know how to read at the time. The few pieces that were translated into Latin did survive. Eventually, they found a new audience of eager students hungry to discover the teachings of the Greek philosophers, and Aristotle made a comeback. By the 12th and 13th centuries, those who rediscovered Aristotle delved into his philosophies and teachings. He became known as "the philosopher." His regard was so high that his words and thoughts rose above all other philosophers that came before and after him.

Dante

When the European Renaissance took hold, educated men and women began to study and appreciate Aristotle. They considered him to be the one with all the answers to how the world worked. Poets such as Dante and Chaucer wrote stories, comedies, and fables about Aristotle, his life, and his teachings.

Christians and Muslims were not the only theologians who adopted what is now called Aristotelianism in their world outlook. Jewish philosophers like Moses Maimonides based their scholastic philosophies on Aristotle's teachings. Moses Maimonides considered Aristotle the "chief of philosophers" and the greatest philosopher ever.

Later, scientists such as William Harvey of England, who made discoveries in the study of anatomy and physiology, and Galileo Galilei, the first astronomer, physicist, and engineer, each established theories that contradicted many of Aristotle's findings. And what they discovered changed how we viewed the world. Aristotle's view of life no longer had the impact it once had. His ideologies, scientific discoveries, and teachings were no longer gospel. Many people in the world started to move forward, and Aristotle no longer had all the answers.

By the 19th century and through the early 20th century, many philosophers, scholars, and scientists continued to use Aristotle, not necessarily for the answers to various questions but as a frame for their concepts and ideologies. They would jump off of what Aristotle wrote and take it further.

The German philosopher Fredrich Neitzche considered himself a true student of Aristotle. He based much of his political philosophy on Aristotle's political science concepts.

Friedrich Nietzsche

English philosopher George Boole based his theories of Logic on Aristotle's works on Logic. But he gave Aristotle's concepts of the study of Logic more of a foundation, thus bringing Aristotle's ideas on the discipline of Logic into a more modern viewpoint.

Then there was Charles Darwin.

Darwin expressed how important he felt Aristotle's work and contribution to the study of biology were. He described this in his famous work, "On the Origins of Species." In Darwin's work, he presented his scientific theory on evolutionary biology. He traced his concepts directly to Aristotle's early work on biology, which he conducted on the island of Lesbos hundreds of years before Darwin's groundbreaking work on evolution.

Charles Darwin

Another very influential philosopher of the 19th century was Karl Marx. Marx considered Aristotle to be a genius and a "giant thinker." His political ideologies were based on Aristotle's work on political science. Aristotle's concepts helped Marx create his doctrines on working-class political reforms such as Socialism and Communism.

Aristotle highly influenced authors like James Joyce and Ayn Rand. Each considered Aristotle to be the greatest philosopher of all time. You can see where some of Aristotle's feelings about society emanate from their manuscripts and novels.

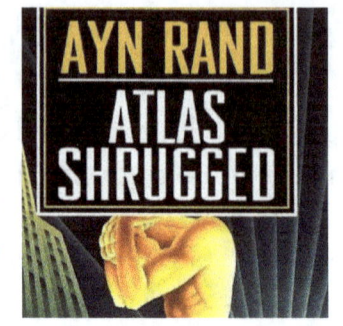

There came a time in the 20th century when it became fashionable to criticize Aristotle and his concepts. These criticisms looked at the flaws in Aristotle's observations and how he viewed the world. Science was evolving dramatically, and people's ideas and philosophies differed distinctly from Aristotle's. Aristotle remained a powerful force, but his work had a different impact. Now philosophers did not piggyback on his concepts but used them to challenge the intellects of modern-day philosophers, scientists, scholars, and writers, which is likely what Aristotle would have preferred. If you go by the way Aristotle modeled his ideologies on teaching, he would have selected not to be exalted by others who contemplated his works but instead to challenge the intellect and ideas of those who chose to be his students. It was why he was so prolific and monumental in his thoughts and teachings.

To this day, Aristotle endures in his thoughts, philosophies, concepts, and teachings. They continue to stand the test of time, even though his ideas were conceived without the benefit of today's scientific equipment. He is one of the most famous philosophers and is still revered. Aristotle continues to influence new generations of thinkers. He remains a good starting point for most intellects who want to understand specific concepts better. For this reason, his influence is as strong as ever.

- *After reading some of Aristotle's concepts, do you find that you can relate to any of them?*

- *Could you use some of his works to help you develop your ideologies or concepts?*

- *What impressions do you have of Aristotle after reading more about his life and his philosophies and concepts?*

———◆———

Some Takeaways about Aristotle

"Learning is not child's play; we cannot learn without pain."

- Aristotle

Aristotle's many achievements are remarkable. He was the first genuine scientist in history. He was the first biologist and zoologist. He elevated the study of Logic by showing the difference between observation and theory. He created a variety of scientific and philosophical disciplines, with many of these being related to one another. He charted various governments and theories and was the first person to make politics a science.

Aristotle was the first professor to organize his lectures. He was the first teacher to create a syllabus, yet another invention to thank him for giving us. His university, The Lyceum, was the first research institution. It was where scholars of his time would gather to collaborate on various types of scientific and philosophical work.

Aristotle wrote thousands of pages of material throughout his life. He taught some of the most outstanding leaders of his day. His work was placed in a research library that has lasted through the ages. It was at first utilized by his colleagues and students. It was handed down to scholars, philosophers, theologians, professors, scientists, and the average man and woman who wanted to seek more excellence and knowledge.

Aristotle's philosophies, discoveries, and teachings have lasted for the last couple of millennia. He is still considered one of the greatest Western philosophers, and almost everyone can take something of value from his works, philosophies, and teachings. It is up to you how you will utilize what you have discovered on your journey to becoming a philosopher and great thinker, following in the realm of Aristotle's teachings and ideologies. You will be in great company with many of the great thinkers of our time, who were also influenced by Aristotle, who was indeed the philosopher's philosopher.

Bibliography

"Aristotle." *Encyclopædia Britannica*, Encyclopædia Britannica, https://www.britannica.com/biography/Aristotle. Accessed 16 Jan. 2023.

"Aristotle Quotes (Author of The Nicomachean Ethics)." *Goodreads | Meet Your Next Favorite Book*, https://www.goodreads.com/author/quotes/2192.Aristotle. Accessed 16 Jan. 2023.

Christopher. "Aristotle (Stanford Encyclopedia of Philosophy)." *Stanford Encyclopedia of Philosophy*, https://plato.stanford.edu/entries/aristotle/. Accessed 16 Jan. 2023.

Contributors to Wikimedia projects. "Aristotle - Wikipedia." *Wikipedia, the Free Encyclopedia*, Wikimedia Foundation, Inc., 11 Nov. 2001, https://en.wikipedia.org/wiki/Aristotle.

---. "Four Causes - Wikipedia." *Wikipedia, the Free Encyclopedia*, Wikimedia Foundation, Inc., 28 June 2005, https://en.wikipedia.org/wiki/Four_causes.

Marc, S. "Aristotle's Metaphysics (Stanford Encyclopedia of Philosophy)." *Stanford Encyclopedia of Philosophy*, https://plato.stanford.edu/entries/aristotle-metaphysics/. Accessed 16 Jan. 2023.

Trumpeter, Amy. "Aristotle's Four Causes - Material, Formal, Efficient and Final." *Philosophyzer*, 31 Oct. 2012, https://www.philosophyzer.com/aristotles-four-causes/.

"▷ Aristotle's Four Causes | Science Philosophy." *Simply Philosophy | Think Critically*, https://simplyphilosophy.org/study/aristotles-four-causes/. Accessed 16 Jan. 2023.

"Aristotle: Biology | Internet Encyclopedia of Philosophy." *Internet Encyclopedia of Philosophy | An Encyclopedia of Philosophy Articles Written by Professional Philosophers.*, https://iep.utm.edu/aristotle-biology/. Accessed 16 Jan. 2023.

"Aristotle: Metaphysics | Internet Encyclopedia of Philosophy." *Internet Encyclopedia of Philosophy | An Encyclopedia of Philosophy Articles Written by Professional Philosophers.*, https://iep.utm.edu/aristotle-metaphysics/. Accessed 16 Jan. 2023.

Contributors to Wikimedia projects. "Aristotle's Biology - Wikipedia." *Wikipedia, the Free Encyclopedia*, Wikimedia Foundation, Inc., 30 Nov. 2015, https://en.wikipedia.org/wiki/Aristotle%27s_biology.

---. "Metaphysics (Aristotle) - Wikipedia." *Wikipedia, the Free Encyclopedia*, Wikimedia Foundation, Inc., 1 Sept. 2005, https://en.wikipedia.org/wiki/Metaphysics_(Aristotle).

James. "Aristotle's Biology (Stanford Encyclopedia of Philosophy)." *Stanford Encyclopedia of Philosophy*, https://plato.stanford.edu/entries/aristotle-biology/. Accessed 16 Jan. 2023.

Marc, S. "Aristotle's Metaphysics (Stanford Encyclopedia of Philosophy)." *Stanford Encyclopedia of Philosophy*, https://plato.stanford.edu/entries/aristotle-metaphysics/. Accessed 16 Jan. 2023.

"Aristotle." *Encyclopædia Britannica*, Encyclopædia Britannica, https://www.britannica.com/topic/history-of-logic/Aristotle. Accessed 16 Jan. 2023.

"Aristotle Views On The Soul And Body - Free Essay Example - Edubirdie." *Edubirdie*, https://edubirdie.com/examples/aristotle-views-on-the-soul-and-body/. Accessed 16 Jan. 2023.

"Aristotle's View on the Relationship Between Soul and Body | Free Essay Example." *StudyCorgi.Com*, https://studycorgi.com/aristotles-view-on-the-relationship-between-soul-and-body/. Accessed 16 Jan. 2023.

Contributors to Wikimedia projects. "Liar Paradox - Wikipedia." *Wikipedia, the Free Encyclopedia*, Wikimedia Foundation, Inc., 13 Oct. 2001, https://en.wikipedia.org/wiki/Liar_paradox.

"Philosophy of Mind of Aristotle." *Encyclopædia Britannica*, Encyclopædia Britannica, https://www.britannica.com/biography/Aristotle/Philosophy-of-mind. Accessed 16 Jan. 2023.

Robin. "Aristotle's Logic (Stanford Encyclopedia of Philosophy)." *Stanford Encyclopedia of Philosophy*, https://plato.stanford.edu/entries/aristotle-logic/index.html. Accessed 16 Jan. 2023.

"▷ Aristotle's Logic | Logic Philosophy." *Simply Philosophy | Think Critically*, https://simplyphilosophy.org/study/aristotles-logic/. Accessed 16 Jan. 2023.

"Aristotle and Education – Infed.Org:" *Infed*, https://infed.org/mobi/aristotle-and-education/. Accessed 16 Jan. 2023.

"Aristotle's Political Science - Jack Miller Center." *Jack Miller Center*, https://www.facebook.com/EducationForCitizenship/, https://jackmillercenter.org/cd-resources/aristotles-political-science/. Accessed 16 Jan. 2023.

"Aristotle's Theory And Philosophy Of Education - Free Essay Example - Edubirdie." *Edubirdie*, https://edubirdie.com/examples/aristotles-theory-and-philosophy-of-education/. Accessed 16 Jan. 2023.

Contributors to Wikimedia projects. "Politics (Aristotle) - Wikipedia." *Wikipedia, the Free Encyclopedia*, Wikimedia Foundation, Inc., 4 Apr. 2005, https://en.wikipedia.org/wiki/Politics_(Aristotle).

Fred. "Aristotle's Political Theory (Stanford Encyclopedia of Philosophy)." *Stanford Encyclopedia of Philosophy*, https://plato.stanford.edu/entries/aristotle-politics/. Accessed 16 Jan. 2023.

"Political Theory of Aristotle." *Encyclopædia Britannica*, Encyclopædia Britannica, https://www.britannica.com/biography/Aristotle/Political-theory. Accessed 16 Jan. 2023.

Adhikari, Saugat. "Top 10 Contributions of Aristotle - Ancient History Lists." *Ancient History Lists*, 28 Mar. 2017, https://www.ancienthistorylists.com/greek-history/top-10-contributions-of-aristotle/.

Admin. "What Did Aristotle Influence? – Sage-Answer." *Sage-Answer – Just Clear Tips and Lifehacks for Every Day*, 10 Sept. 2020, https://sage-answer.com/what-did-aristotle-influence/.

Carlos. "Alexander the Great Was Aristotle's Greatest Achievement." *The Presence of Everything | Carlos | Substack*, The Presence of Everything, 21 Sept. 2021, https://squarecircle.substack.com/p/alexander-the-great-was-aristotles.

Centre, Apeiron. "Aristotle's Influence on Alexander the Great's Political Thought — Apeiron Centre." *Apeiron Centre*, Apeiron Centre, 10 June 2019, https://apeironcentre.org/aristotles-influence-on-alexander-the-greats-political-thought/.

Contributors to Wikimedia projects. "List of Writers Influenced by Aristotle - Wikipedia." *Wikipedia, the Free Encyclopedia*, Wikimedia Foundation, Inc., 17 May 2009,

https://en.wikipedia.org/wiki/List_of_writers_influenced_by_Aristotle.

"How Did Aristotle Influence Subsequent Philosophy and Science?" *Encyclopædia Britannica*, Encyclopædia Britannica, https://www.britannica.com/question/How-did-Aristotle-influence-subsequent-philosophy-and-science. Accessed 16 Jan. 2023.

Mark, Joshua J. "Aristotle - World History Encyclopedia." *World History Encyclopedia*, https://www.worldhistory.org#organization, 22 May 2019, https://www.worldhistory.org/aristotle/.

Book Illustrations

Illustration 172668859 © Naci Yavuz | Dreamstime.com

llustration 259580507 © Naci Yavuz | Dreamstime.com**rediting the author!**

Illustration 157529855 © Naci Yavuz | Dreamstime.com

Illustration 163084564 © Patrick Guenette | Dreamstime.com

Illustration 197397980 © Matias Del Carmine | Dreamstime.com

Illustration 19733620 © Sifis Diamantidis | Dreamstime.com

Illustration 149239055 © Lineartestpilot | Dreamstime.com

Illustration 18445036 © Vyacheslav Biryukov | Dreamstime.com

Illustration 192717002 © Rawf88 | Dreamstime.com

Illustration 168647714 © Maciej Sojka | Dreamstime.com

Illustration 17576231 © Dimdimich | Dreamstime.com

Illustration 79350253 © ArchitectureVIZ | Dreamstime.com

Illustration 6649856 © Jiri Flogel | Dreamstime.com

Illustration 212303865 © Ruslan Nesterenko | Dreamstime.com

Illustration 212303865 © Ruslan Nesterenko | Dreamstime.com

Illustration 61165835 © Alexander Pokusay | Dreamstime.com

Illustration 243969702 © Passengerz | Dreamstime.com

Illustration 186963268 © Biblebox | Dreamstime.com

Illustration 67824082 © Kittanate Rittipornpasit | Dreamstime.com

Illustration 114575708 © Boldurevaol | Dreamstime.com

Illustration 20384826 © Nicku | Dreamstime.com

Illustration 209276037 © Naci Yavuz | Dreamstime.com

Illustration 249219917 © Niall Wiggan | Dreamstime.com

Illustration 132219277 © Timea Adel Bajko | Dreamstime.com

Illustration 205361231 © Sensvector | Dreamstime.com

Illustration 205751525 © Evgenii Naumov | Dreamstime.comcrediting the author!

Illustration 108155763 © Miaoumiaou | Dreamstime.com

Illustration 63188167 © Steve Estvanik | Dreamstime.com

Illustration 189408636 © Ivona17 | Dreamstime.com

Illustration 218569669 © Passengerz | Dreamstime.com

Illustration 23973840 © Nilikha | Dreamstime.com

Illustration 36307176 © Artistashmita | Dreamstime.comediting the author!

Illustration 49303859 © Jorgenmac | Dreamstime.com

Illustration 213374 © Rolffimages | Dreamstime.com

Illustration 135302744 © Artur Szczybylo | Dreamstime.com

Illustration 240783775 / Election © Tarikvision | Dreamstime.com

Illustration 217186207 © Logan81 | Dreamstime.com

Illustration 138268771 © Mariia Domnikova | Dreamstime.com

If you liked this book, please leave a review on

Amazon, Barnes and Noble, and Smashwords

Please also read our other books in the

Be a Great Thinker Series:

Book 1 – Introduction to Critical Thinking

Book 2 – Socrates – Man, Myth, and Teacher

Book 3 – Plato – The Father of Western Philosophy

The Be a Great Thinker book series is found at your favorite online bookstore.

About the Author

Adrienne Roth is passionate about writing and philosophy and critical thinking. She desires to have all people, no matter their age or background learn about philosophy, the great philosophers, and how to be critical thinkers. Understanding philosophers like Aristotle, Plato, Socrates, and other brilliant minds, is the key to finding the answers while unlocking the mysteries of the world. She is glad you have chosen to be part of the journey to becoming a great thinker.